Music
Practice
Diary

snapping turtle

Date: **25 July**

Scale: **D major**

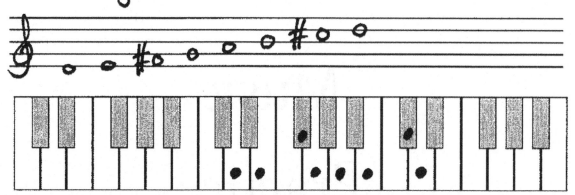

Pages	Exercise or Repertoire	M	T	W	T	F	S	S
15	Exercise 10	✓		✓	✓			
16-17	Exercise 11		✓		✓			
	Song 1	✓			✓			
	Song 2	✓	✓		✓			
	Song 3			✓	✓			

Don't give up. The beginning is always the hardest. Life rewards those who work hard at it.

- Unknown

Music Terms: **Staccato-**
♪ ♪ **short and detached**

Notes:
Please note, no lesson first week of September

Next lesson: **1 Aug 11.30am**

My Goals:

Prepare 3 songs from memory for Annual Concert (November)

My Achievements:

completed Song 1 from memory

played G major scale RH & LH & together.

I need to work on:

left hand ostinato in Song 2

fingering for D major scale

Practice Song 3 at half speed

Date: _____

Scale:_____

_____
_____
_____
_____
_____

Pages	Exercise or Repertoire	M	T	W	T	F	S	S

Don't give up. The beginning is always the hardest. Life rewards those who work hard at it.
- Unknown

Music Terms:

Notes:

Next lesson:

My Goals:

My Achievements:

I need to work on:

Date: _____

Scale:_____

Pages	Exercise or Repertoire	M	T	W	T	F	S	S

To study music, we must learn the rules. To create music, we must break them.
— Nadia Boulanger

Music Terms:

Notes:

Next lesson:

My Goals:

My Achievements:

I need to work on:

Date: _____

Scale:_____

_____
_____
_____
_____
_____

Pages	Exercise or Repertoire	M	T	W	T	F	S	S

There will never come a time when you don't have to practice.
—J.J. Johnson

Music Terms:

Notes:

Next lesson:

My Goals:

My Achievements:

I need to work on:

Date: _____

Scale:_____

_____
_____
_____
_____
_____

Pages	Exercise or Repertoire	M	T	W	T	F	S	S

Stage fright needs to be confronted and experienced in order to be conquered.
— Eloise Ristad

Music Terms:

Notes:

Next lesson:

My Goals:

My Achievements:

I need to work on:

Date: _____

Scale: _____

Pages	Exercise or Repertoire	M	T	W	T	F	S	S

Every day you don't practice, you're one day further from being good.
— Ben Hogan

Music Terms:

Notes:

Next lesson:

My Goals:

My Achievements:

I need to work on:

Date: _____

Scale:_____

Pages	Exercise or Repertoire	M	T	W	T	F	S	S

By failing to prepare, you are preparing to fail.
— Benjamin Franklin

Music Terms:

Notes:

Next lesson:

My Goals:

My Achievements:

I need to work on:

Date: _____

Scale: _____

Pages	Exercise or Repertoire	M	T	W	T	F	S	S

Motivation gets you going and habit gets you there.
— Zig Ziglar

Music Terms:

Notes:

Next lesson:

My Goals:

My Achievements:

I need to work on:

Date: _____

Scale: _____

Pages	Exercise or Repertoire	M	T	W	T	F	S	S

There is no such thing as failure, only feedback
— David Buswell

Music Terms:

Notes:

Next lesson:

My Goals:

My Achievements:

I need to work on:

Date: _____

Scale: _____

Pages	Exercise or Repertoire	M	T	W	T	F	S	S

The difference between knowledge and skill is practice.
— Holly Marie Simmers

Music Terms:

Notes:

Next lesson:

My Goals:

My Achievements:

I need to work on:

Date: _____

Scale:_____

Pages	Exercise or Repertoire	M	T	W	T	F	S	S

Learning never exhausts the mind.
— Leonardo da Vinci

Music Terms:

Notes:

Next lesson:

My Goals:

My Achievements:

I need to work on:

Date: _____

Scale: _____

Pages	Exercise or Repertoire	M	T	W	T	F	S	S

The beautiful thing about learning is that nobody can take it away from you.
— B.B. King

Music Terms:

Notes:

Next lesson:

My Goals:

My Achievements:

I need to work on:

Date: _____

Scale:_____

Pages	Exercise or Repertoire	M	T	W	T	F	S	S

When you are not practicing, remember, someone somewhere is practicing, and when you meet him he will win.
— Ed Macauley

Music Terms:

Notes:

Next lesson:

My Goals:

My Achievements:

I need to work on:

Date: _____

Scale: _____

Pages	Exercise or Repertoire	M	T	W	T	F	S	S

The best way for a student to get out of difficulty is to go through it
— Aristotle

Music Terms:

Notes:

Next lesson:

My Goals:

My Achievements:

I need to work on:

Date: _____

Scale: _____

Pages	Exercise or Repertoire	M	T	W	T	F	S	S

It is important to practice at the speed of no mistakes
— Lucinda Mackworth-Young

Music Terms:

Notes:

Next lesson:

My Goals:

My Achievements:

I need to work on:

Date: _____

Scale: _____

Pages	Exercise or Repertoire	M	T	W	T	F	S	S

Music should make you feel good.
– Mark James Klepaski

Music Terms:

Notes:

Next lesson:

My Goals:

My Achievements:

I need to work on:

Date: _____

Scale:_____

Pages	Exercise or Repertoire	M	T	W	T	F	S	S

Those at the top of the mountain didn't fall there.
— Unknown

Music Terms:

Notes:

Next lesson:

My Goals:

My Achievements:

I need to work on:

Date: _____

Scale: _____

Pages	Exercise or Repertoire	M	T	W	T	F	S	S

Your habits in the practice room make you the musician that you are.
— The Musician's Way

Music Terms:

Notes:

Next lesson:

My Goals:

My Achievements:

I need to work on:

Date: _____

Scale:_____

Pages	Exercise or Repertoire	M	T	W	T	F	S	S

All growth depends upon activity. There is no development physically or intellectually without effort, and effort means work.
— Calvin Coolidge

Music Terms:

Notes:

Next lesson:

My Goals:

My Achievements:

I need to work on:

Date: _____

Scale: _____

Pages	Exercise or Repertoire	M	T	W	T	F	S	S

Try a little harder to be a little better.
— Gordon B. Hinckley

Music Terms:

Notes:

Next lesson:

My Goals:

My Achievements:

I need to work on:

Date: _____

Scale: _____

Pages	Exercise or Repertoire	M	T	W	T	F	S	S

It's not necessarily the amount of time you spend at practice that counts; it's what you put into the practice.
— Eric Lindros

Music Terms:

Notes:

Next lesson:

My Goals:

My Achievements:

I need to work on:

Date: _____

Scale: _____

Pages	Exercise or Repertoire	M	T	W	T	F	S	S

Music washes away from the soul the dust of everyday life.
— Berthold Auerbach

Music Terms:	Notes:
	Next lesson:

My Goals:

My Achievements:

I need to work on:

_____
_____
_____
_____

_____
_____
_____
_____

_____
_____
_____
_____

_____
_____
_____
_____

Date: _____

Scale:_____

Pages	Exercise or Repertoire	M	T	W	T	F	S	S

All great achievements require time.
— Maya Angelou

Music Terms:

Notes:

Next lesson:

My Goals:

My Achievements:

I need to work on:

Date: _____

Scale: _____

Pages	Exercise or Repertoire	M	T	W	T	F	S	S

If you want to become a musician you must practice. There is no other way.
There are no shortcuts.
— Ron Ottley

Music Terms:

Notes:

Next lesson:

My Goals:

My Achievements:

I need to work on:

Date: _____

Scale:_____

Pages	Exercise or Repertoire	M	T	W	T	F	S	S

If you have played "six times wrong, one time right" the problem is not quite corrected.
— William Westney

Music Terms:

Notes:

Next lesson:

My Goals:

My Achievements:

I need to work on:

Date: _____

Scale:_____

Pages	Exercise or Repertoire	M	T	W	T	F	S	S

The word "fail", of course ceases to apply if we know that . .
we are merely gaining information.
— Eloise Ristad

Music Terms:

Notes:

Next lesson:

My Goals:

My Achievements:

I need to work on:

Date: _____

Scale: _____

Pages	Exercise or Repertoire	M	T	W	T	F	S	S

Practice does not make perfect – it makes permanent
— Alexander Libermann

Music Terms:

Notes:

Next lesson:

My Goals:

My Achievements:

I need to work on:

Date: _____

Scale: _____

Pages	Exercise or Repertoire	M	T	W	T	F	S	S

If you can dream it, you can do it.
— Walt Disney

Music Terms:

Notes:

Next lesson:

My Goals:

My Achievements:

I need to work on:

Date: _____

Scale: _____

Pages	Exercise or Repertoire	M	T	W	T	F	S	S

Goals without deadlines are not really goals, but daydreams
— Harvey Snitkin

Music Terms:

Notes:

Next lesson:

My Goals:

My Achievements:

I need to work on:

Date: _____

Scale:_____

Pages	Exercise or Repertoire	M	T	W	T	F	S	S

The big win is when you refuse to settle for average or mediocre.
— Seth Godin

Music Terms:

Notes:

Next lesson:

My Goals:

My Achievements:

I need to work on:

Date: _____

Scale: _____

_____
_____
_____
_____
_____

Pages	Exercise or Repertoire	M	T	W	T	F	S	S

Music can change the world because it can change people.

— Bono

Music Terms:

Notes:

Next lesson:

My Goals:

My Achievements:

I need to work on:

Date: _____

Scale:_____

Pages	Exercise or Repertoire	M	T	W	T	F	S	S

Have a goal. Work towards it. Because there is not a thing more fulfilling than reaping the fruits of your labor.
— Amanda Shivrattan

Music Terms:

Notes:

Next lesson:

My Goals:

My Achievements:

I need to work on:

Date: _____

Scale:_____

Pages	Exercise or Repertoire	M	T	W	T	F	S	S

Practice doesn't make perfect. It just makes you better.
— Tawa Suleman

Music Terms:

Notes:

Next lesson:

My Goals:

My Achievements:

I need to work on:

Date: _____

Scale: _____

Pages	Exercise or Repertoire	M	T	W	T	F	S	S

As you learn a new piece, remember how important it is to learn it accurately
from the beginning.
— Eloise Ristad

Music Terms:

Notes:

Next lesson:

My Goals:

My Achievements:

I need to work on:

Date: _____

Scale: _____

_____
_____
_____
_____
_____

Pages	Exercise or Repertoire	M	T	W	T	F	S	S

The most valuable practice aid is patience.

— Howard Snell

Music Terms:

Notes:

Next lesson:

My Goals:

My Achievements:

I need to work on:

Date: _____

Scale: _____

Pages	Exercise or Repertoire	M	T	W	T	F	S	S

Don't just memorise notes; memorise the feeling of playing them.
— Madeline Bruser

Music Terms:

Notes:

Next lesson:

My Goals:

My Achievements:

I need to work on:

Date: _____

Scale: _____

Pages	Exercise or Repertoire	M	T	W	T	F	S	S

Repetition was never designed to fix problems — it takes what you are doing — good or bad and locks it in.
— Philip Johnston

Music Terms:

Notes:

Next lesson:

My Goals:

My Achievements:

I need to work on:

Date: _____

Scale: _____

Pages	Exercise or Repertoire	M	T	W	T	F	S	S

You've got to learn your instrument. Then, you practice, practice, practice. And then, when you finally get up there on the bandstand, forget all that and just wail.
— Charlie Parker

Music Terms:

Notes:

Next lesson:

My Goals:

My Achievements:

I need to work on:

Date: _____

Scale: _____

Pages	Exercise or Repertoire	M	T	W	T	F	S	S

The more a piece affects our heart, the more easily we remember it.
— Madeline Bruser

Music Terms:

Notes:

Next lesson:

My Goals:

My Achievements:

I need to work on:

Date: _____

Scale: _____

Pages	Exercise or Repertoire	M	T	W	T	F	S	S

Mistakes are immensely useful. They show us where we are
right now and what we need to do next.
— William Westney

Music Terms:	Notes:
	Next lesson:

My Goals:

My Achievements:

I need to work on:

Date: _____

Scale: _____

_____
_____
_____
_____
_____

Pages	Exercise or Repertoire	M	T	W	T	F	S	S

The 'magic number' is the number of times you practice a spot after getting it exactly the way you want it.
— Margaret Elson

Music Terms:

Notes:

Next lesson:

My Goals:

My Achievements:

I need to work on:

Date: _____

Scale: _____

Pages	Exercise or Repertoire	M	T	W	T	F	S	S

If we're not actively making things better, chances are we're making them worse.
— William Westney

Music Terms:

Notes:

Next lesson:

My Goals:

My Achievements:

I need to work on:

Date: _____

Scale: _____

Pages	Exercise or Repertoire	M	T	W	T	F	S	S

Your success depends on how well you develop your ears.
— Harvey Snitkin

Music Terms:

Notes:

Next lesson:

My Goals:

My Achievements:

I need to work on:

Date: _____

Scale:_____

Pages	Exercise or Repertoire	M	T	W	T	F	S	S

*The most crucial ingredient by far for success in music is
what happens in the practice room.*
— William Westney

Music Terms:	Notes:
	Next lesson:

My Goals:

My Achievements:

I need to work on:

Date: _____

Scale: _____

Pages	Exercise or Repertoire	M	T	W	T	F	S	S

How is it that music can, without words, evoke our laughter, our fears,
our highest aspirations?
— Jane Swan

Music Terms:

Notes:

Next lesson:

My Goals:

My Achievements:

I need to work on:

Date: _____

Scale: _____

Pages	Exercise or Repertoire	M	T	W	T	F	S	S

Where words fail, music speaks.
— Hans Christian Andersen

Music Terms:

Notes:

Next lesson:

My Goals:

My Achievements:

I need to work on:

Date: _____

Scale: _____

Pages	Exercise or Repertoire	M	T	W	T	F	S	S

Music expresses that which cannot be put into words and that which cannot remain silent
— Victor Hugo

Music Terms:

Notes:

Next lesson:

My Goals:

My Achievements:

I need to work on:

Date: _____

Scale: _____

Pages	Exercise or Repertoire	M	T	W	T	F	S	S

The pianokeys are black and white
but they sound like a million colors in your mind
— Maria Cristina Mena

Music Terms:

Notes:

Next lesson:

My Goals:

My Achievements:

I need to work on:

Date: _____

Scale: _____

Pages	Exercise or Repertoire	M	T	W	T	F	S	S

If you cannot teach me to fly, teach me to sing.

— J.M. Barrie

Music Terms:

Notes:

Next lesson:

My Goals:

My Achievements:

I need to work on:

Date: _____

Scale: _____

Pages	Exercise or Repertoire	M	T	W	T	F	S	S

After silence, that which comes nearest to expressing the inexpressible is music.
— Aldous Huxley

Music Terms:

Notes:

Next lesson:

My Goals:

My Achievements:

I need to work on:

Date: _____

Scale: _____

Pages	Exercise or Repertoire	M	T	W	T	F	S	S

We are the music makers, and we are the dreamers of dreams.
— Arthur O'Shaughnessy

Music Terms:

Notes:

Next lesson:

My Goals:

My Achievements:

I need to work on:

Date: _____

Scale: _____

_____
_____
_____
_____
_____

Pages	Exercise or Repertoire	M	T	W	T	F	S	S

Music produces a kind of pleasure which human nature cannot do without.
— Confucius

Music Terms:

Notes:

Next lesson:

My Goals:

My Achievements:

I need to work on:

Made in the USA
Middletown, DE
02 October 2023